THE LIFE AND DEATH OF BLING BLING

A STORY OF INNOVATION, PROLIFERATION, REGURGITATION, COMMERCIALIZATION AND BASTARDIZATION

PRESENTED BY MATTHEW VESCOVO — MASTER OF THE OBVIOUS

*O*nce there was a rap group singing about diamonds and jewelry of the large-size variety.

It was clear the crowd agreed...for them too, it was a priority.

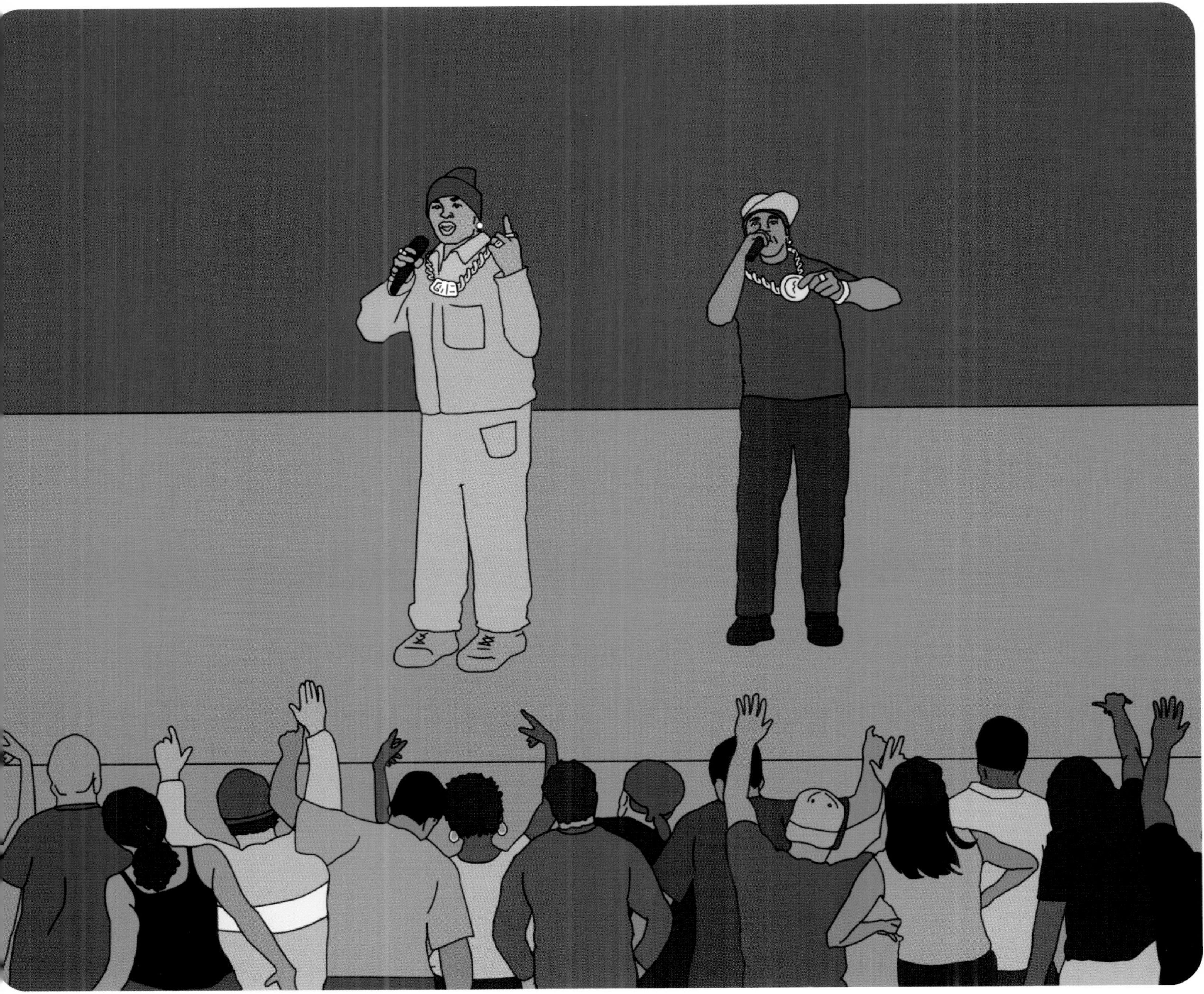

*T*heir love of all that glittered was perfectly summarized when they began to sing...

A simple little two-word chorus that went...
Bling Bling.

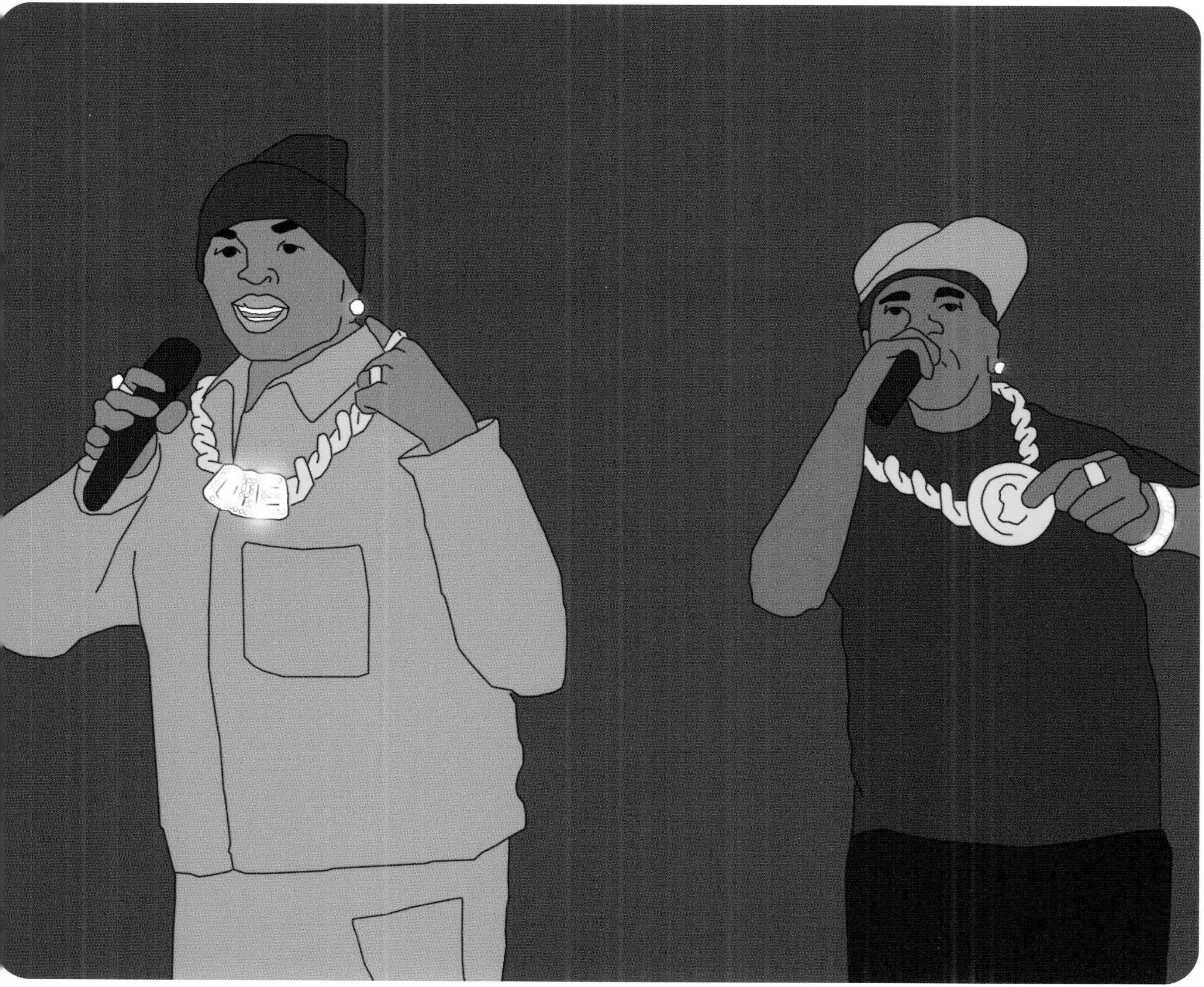

*T*he audience left with more than when they came.

Most lyrics faded, but their memory had one
it was sure to claim.

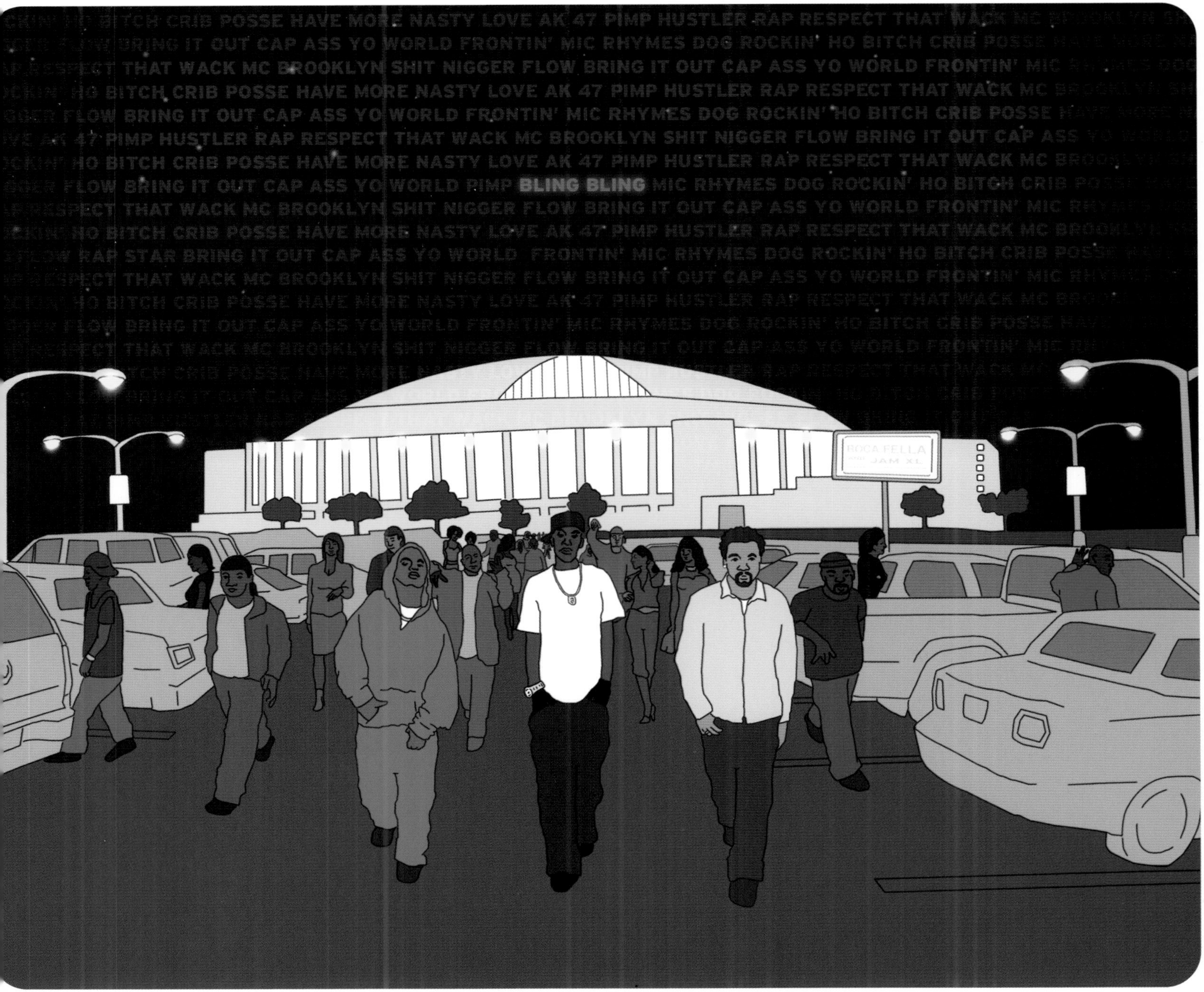
HO BITCH CRIB POSSE HAVE MORE NASTY LOVE AK 47 PIMP HUSTLER RAP RESPECT THAT WACK MC
FLOW BRING IT OUT CAP ASS YO WORLD FRONTIN' MIC RHYMES DOG ROCKIN' HO BITCH CRIB POSSE
RESPECT THAT WACK MC BROOKLYN SHIT NIGGER FLOW BRING IT OUT CAP ASS YO WORLD FRONTIN' MIC
HO BITCH CRIB POSSE HAVE MORE NASTY LOVE AK 47 PIMP HUSTLER RAP RESPECT THAT WACK MC
FLOW BRING IT OUT CAP ASS YO WORLD FRONTIN' MIC RHYMES DOG ROCKIN' HO BITCH CRIB POSSE
AK 47 PIMP HUSTLER RAP RESPECT THAT WACK MC BROOKLYN SHIT NIGGER FLOW BRING IT OUT CAP ASS
HO BITCH CRIB POSSE HAVE MORE NASTY LOVE AK 47 PIMP HUSTLER RAP RESPECT THAT WACK MC
FLOW BRING IT OUT CAP ASS YO WORLD PIMP BLING BLING MIC RHYMES DOG ROCKIN' HO BITCH CRIB
RESPECT THAT WACK MC BROOKLYN SHIT NIGGER FLOW BRING IT OUT CAP ASS YO WORLD FRONTIN' MIC
HO BITCH CRIB POSSE HAVE MORE NASTY LOVE AK 47 PIMP HUSTLER RAP RESPECT THAT WACK MC
RAP STAR BRING IT OUT CAP ASS YO WORLD FRONTIN' MIC RHYMES DOG ROCKIN' HO BITCH CRIB
RESPECT THAT WACK MC BROOKLYN SHIT NIGGER FLOW BRING IT OUT CAP ASS YO WORLD FRONTIN' MIC
HO BITCH CRIB POSSE HAVE MORE NASTY LOVE AK 47 PIMP HUSTLER RAP RESPECT THAT WACK MC
FLOW BRING IT OUT CAP ASS YO WORLD FRONTIN' MIC RHYMES DOG ROCKIN' HO BITCH CRIB POSSE
RESPECT THAT WACK MC BROOKLYN SHIT NIGGER FLOW BRING IT OUT CAP ASS YO WORLD FRONTIN' MIC
ROCA FELLA
JAM XL

$\mathscr{B}$ling Bling had something about it
that felt so fresh...and so right.

No one realized, but a new urban phrase
was birthed that very night.

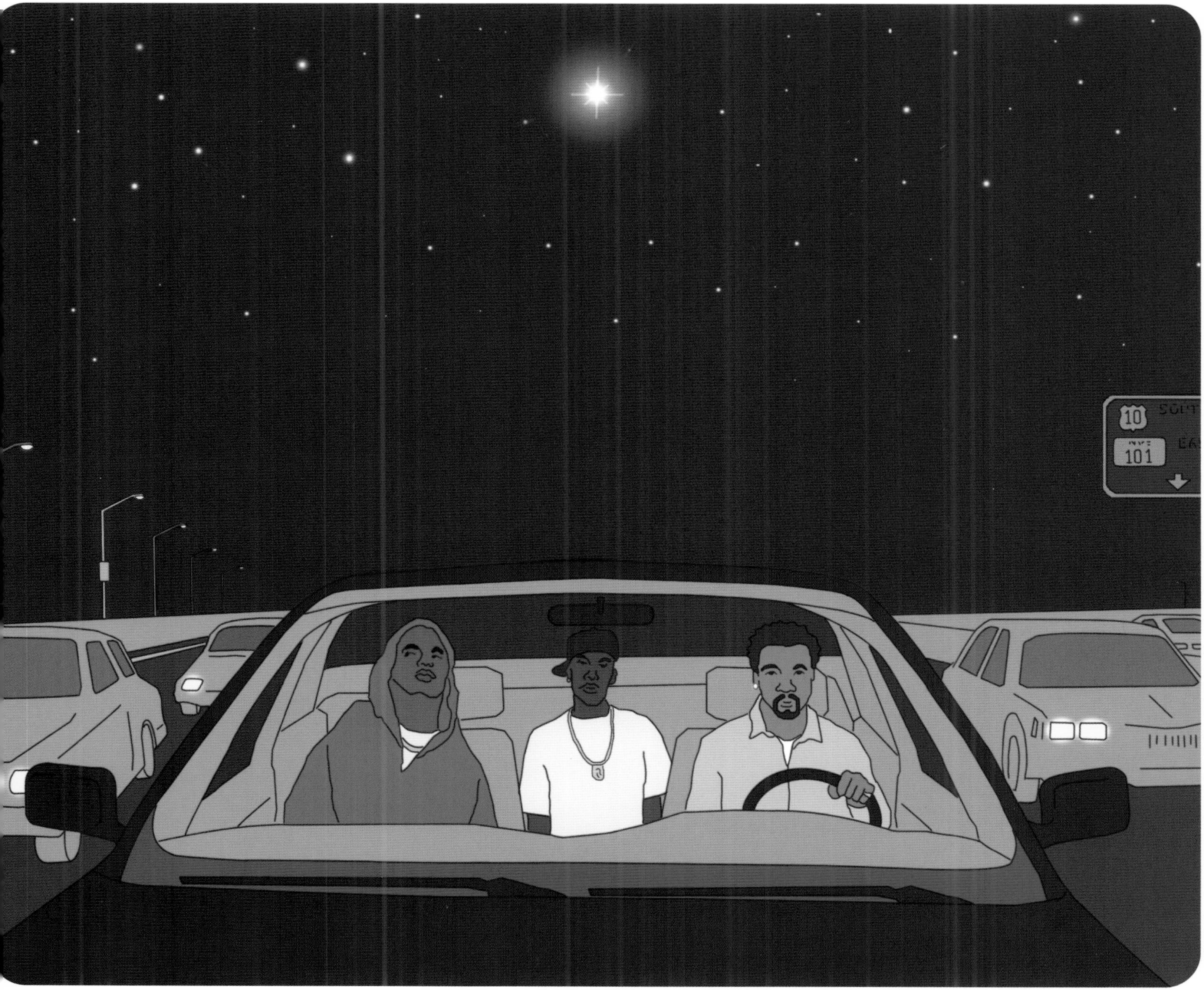
10
101

*T*hey all went their separate ways:
home, job, or to hang with a friend.

Carrying a new weapon in their verbal arsenal...
they were about to start a trend.

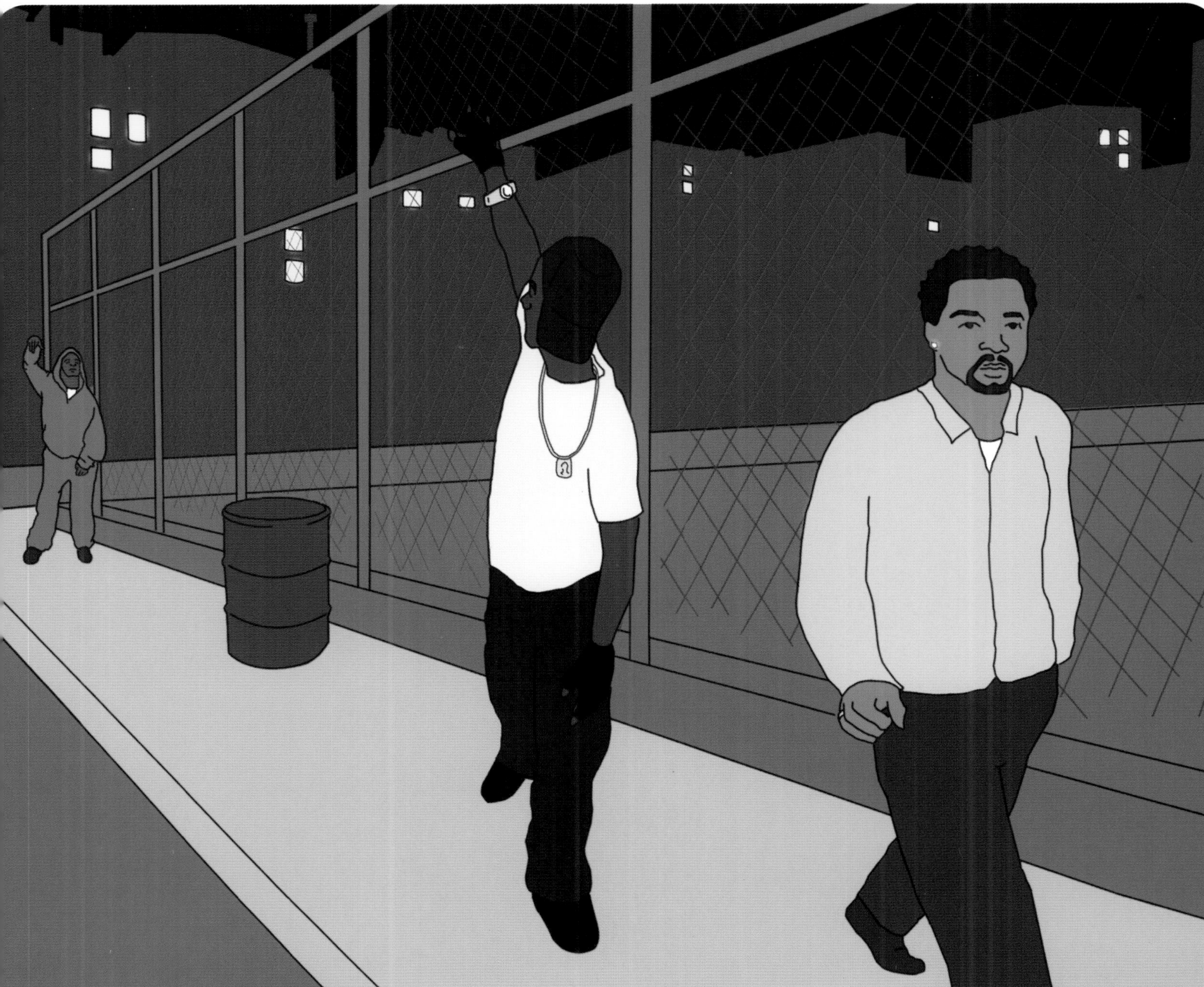

*F*irst time they used it, probably seemed like no big thing.

They just pointed to their diamond studs
and said…"Bling Bling."

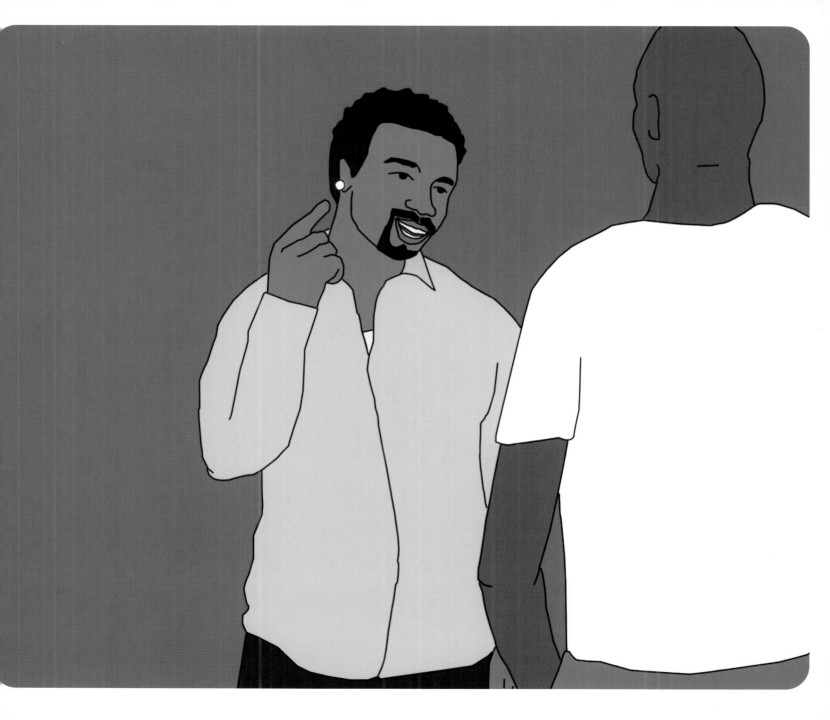

Where the phrase came from no one seemed to notice.

There was one guy who claimed,
"I think it was some dude named Otis."

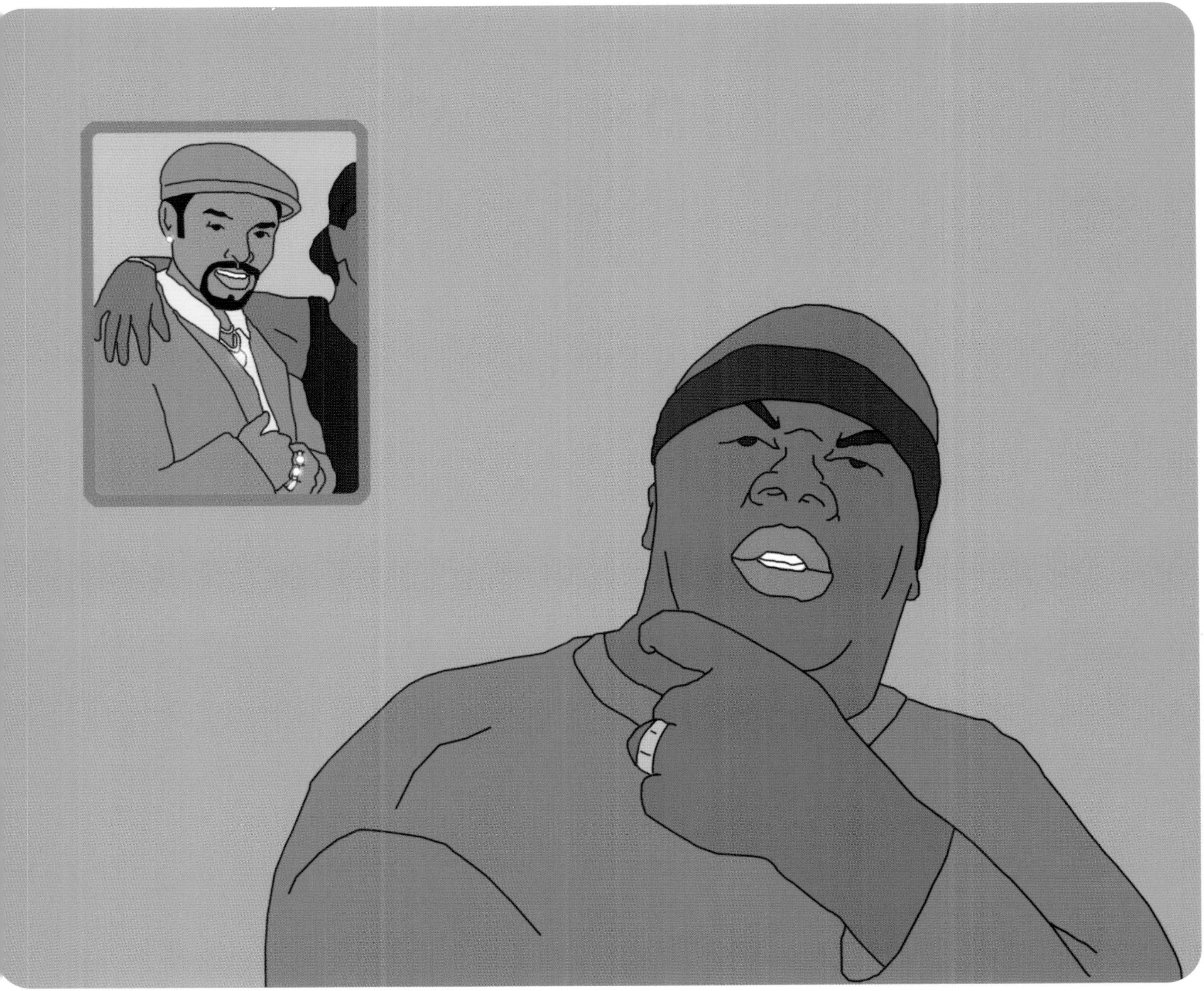

*B*ut where it started mattered not, only where it went.

An urban game of telephone...
(Bling Bling)...(Bling Bling)...calls were being sent.

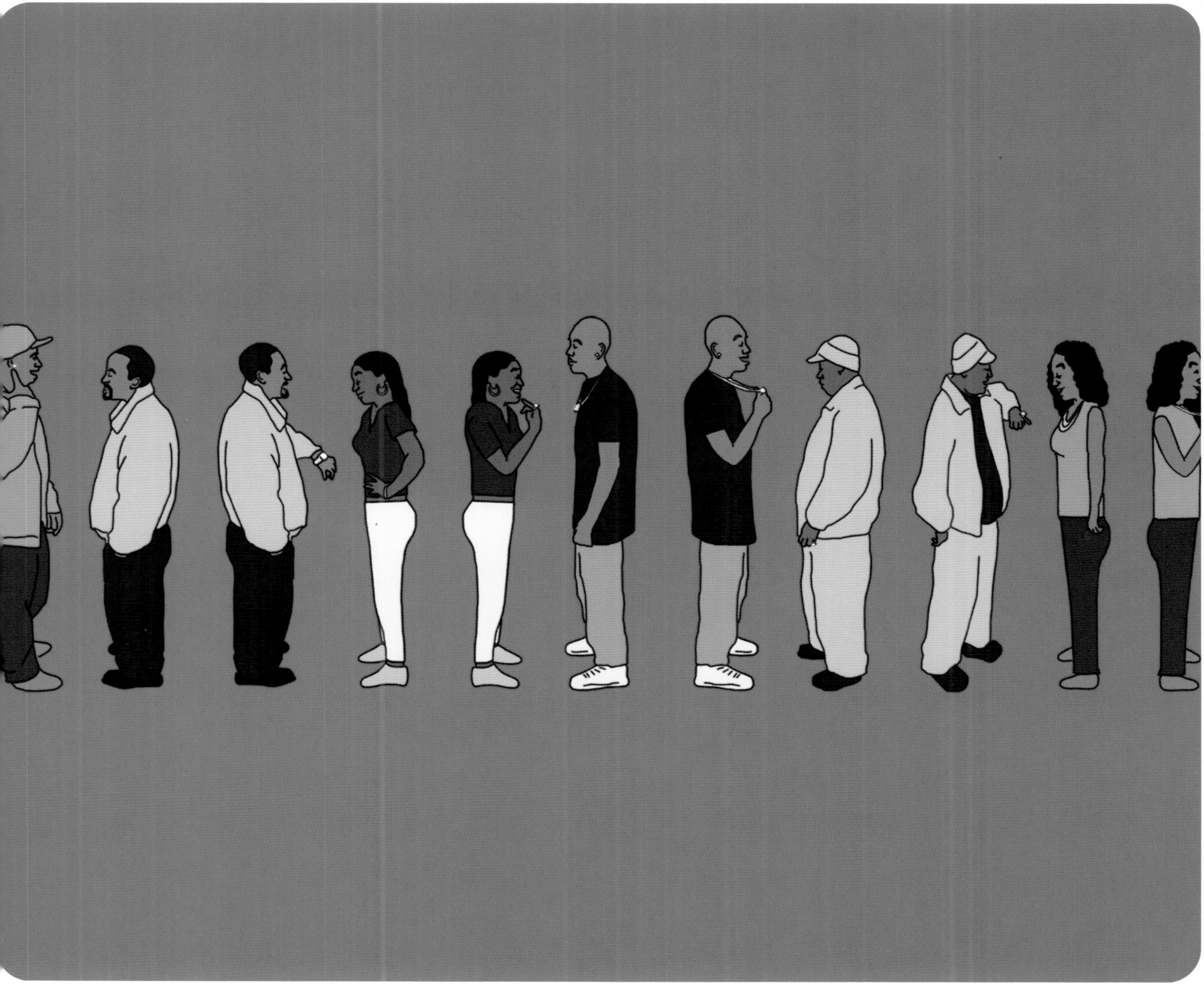

A club was now forming...exclusivity intended.

From homey to homey...membership extended.

◇ ◇

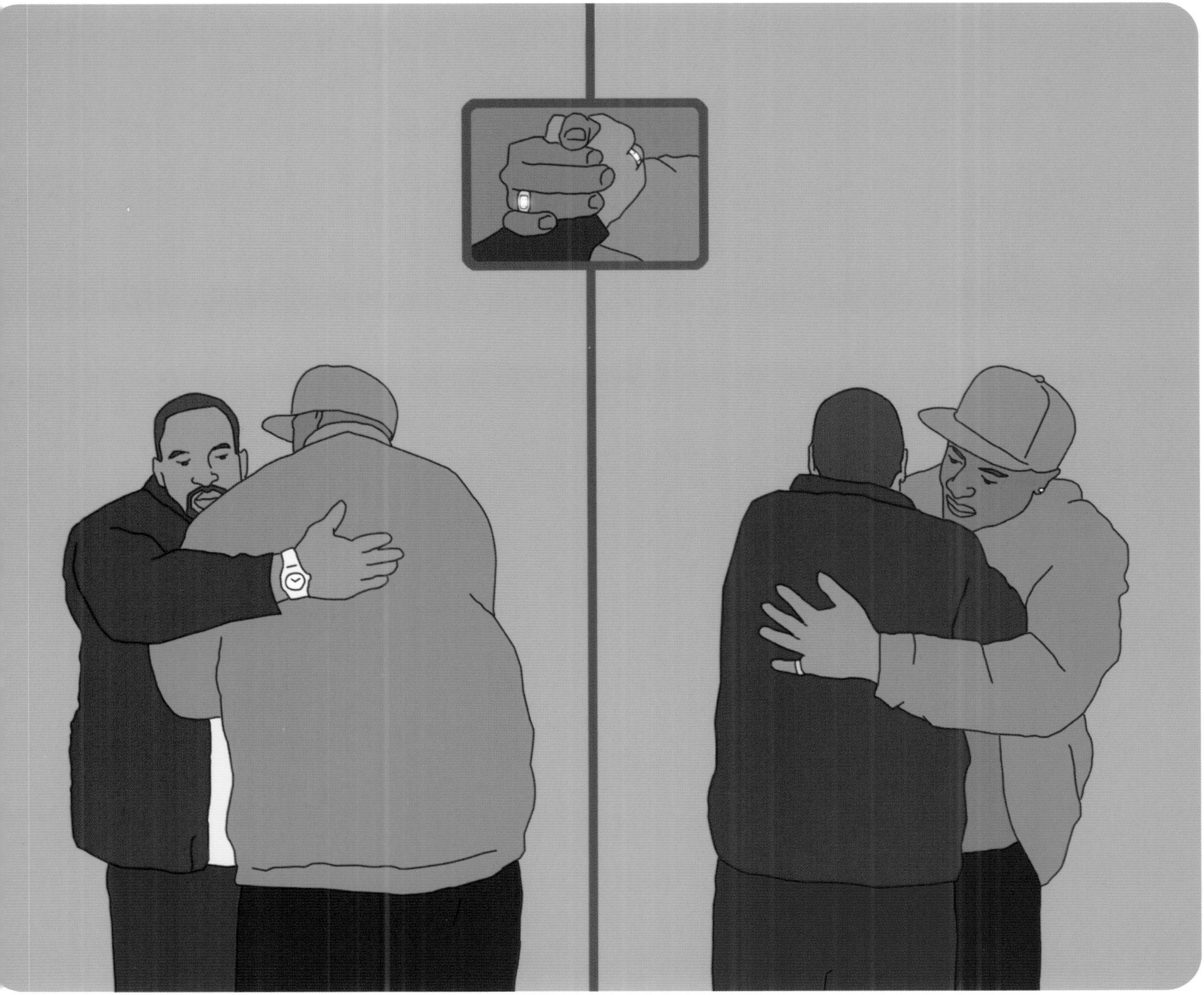

The same exact cadence, tone, pitch and ring.

Like one voice, they all said…"Bling Bling."

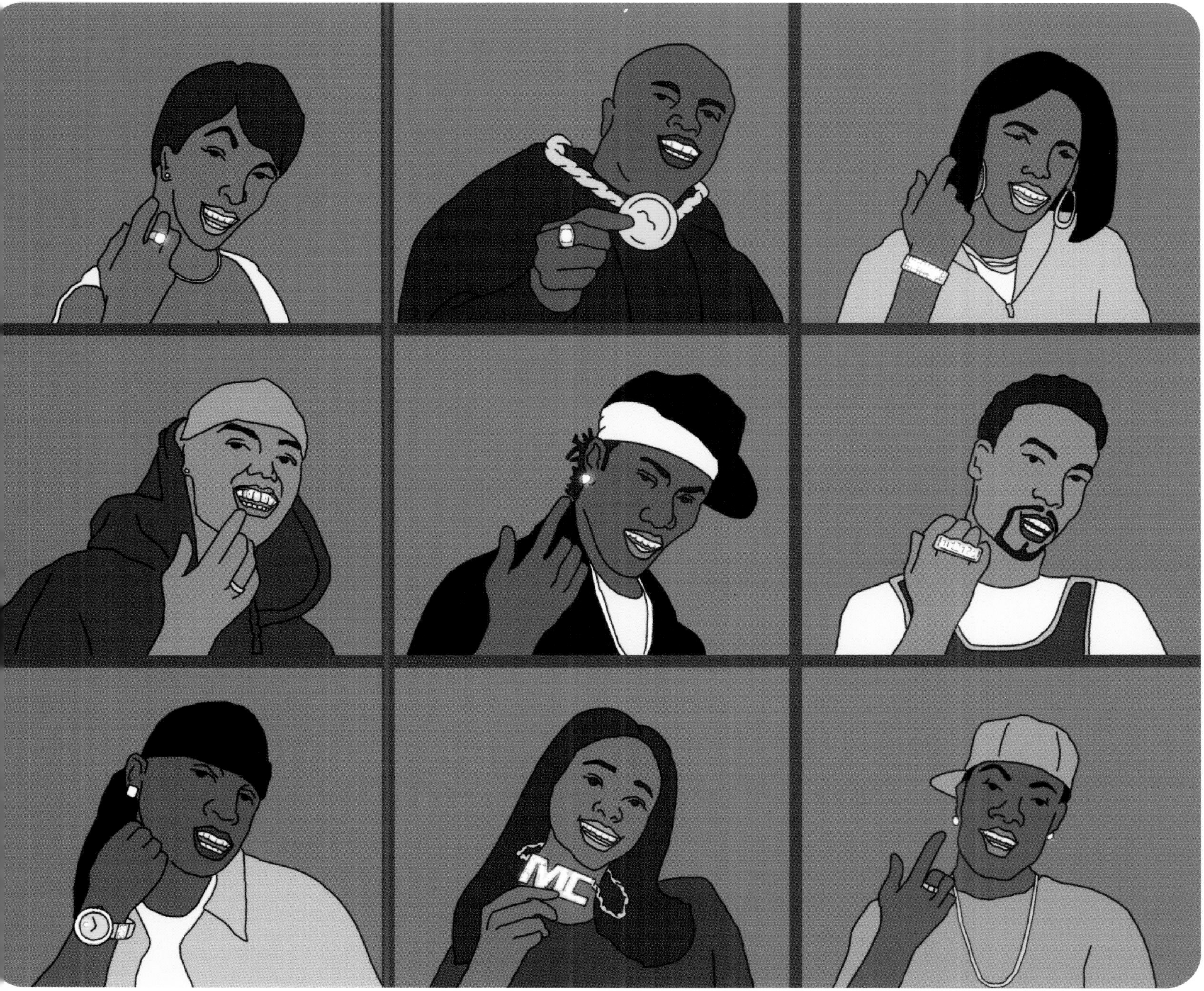
MC

*A*lmost all saved it for those in the know.

But some knew not better...
to keep it on the down low.

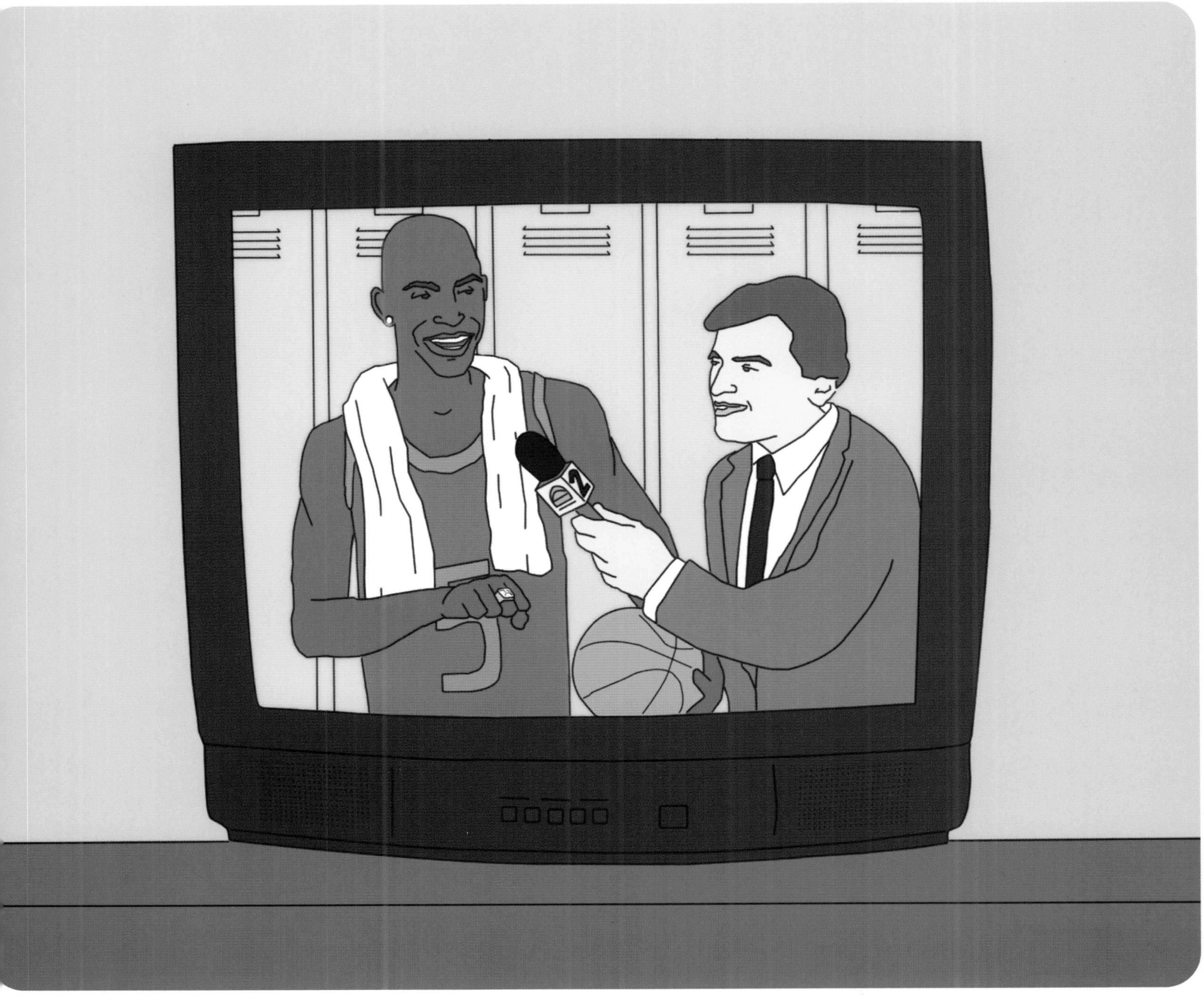

*A*nd thus it spread quicker and grew and grew.

'Til the inevitable happened,
someone heard it who wasn't supposed to.

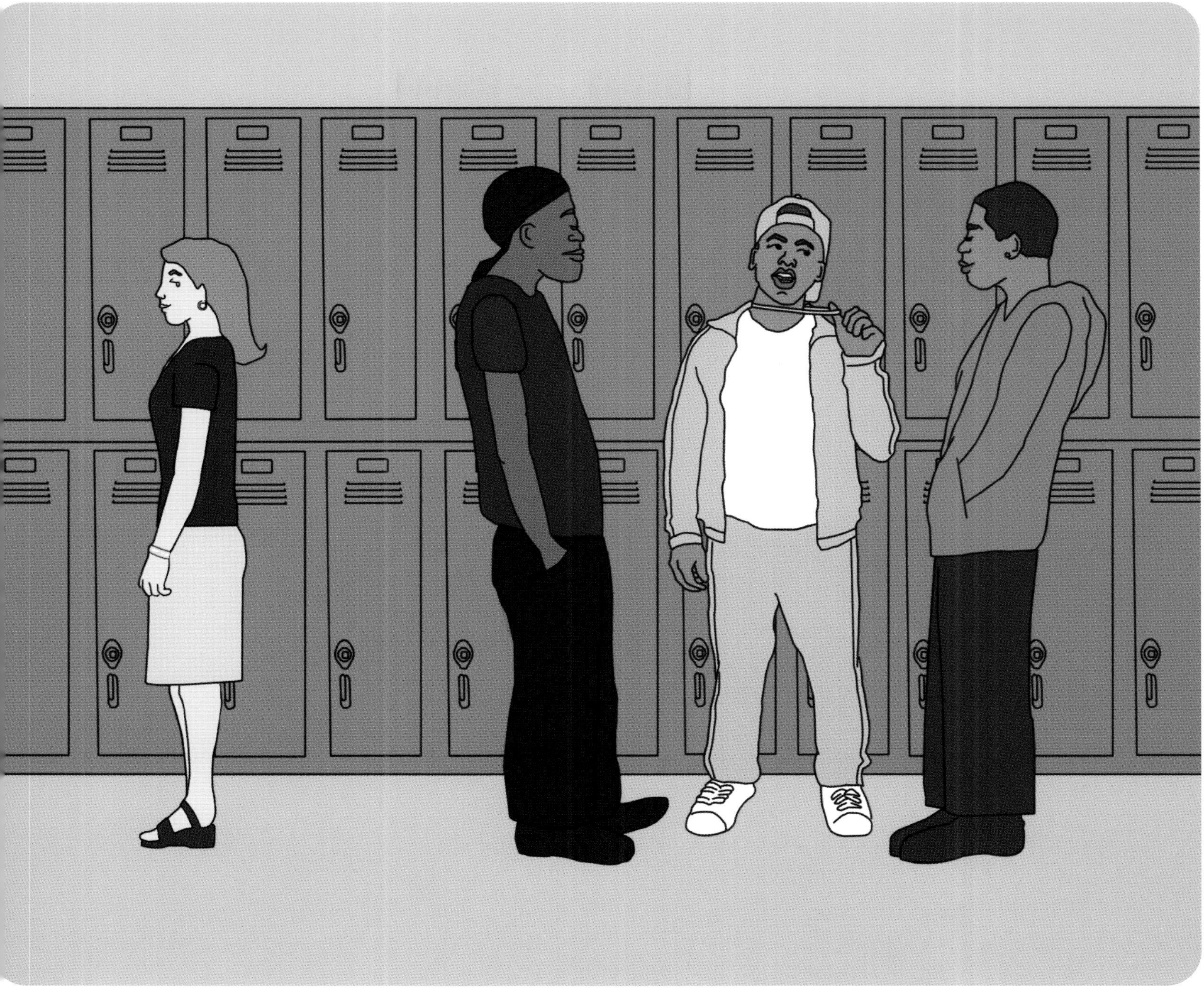

*S*tanding within earshot she had picked up just enough.

Finally, sounding "street" wouldn't be all that tough.

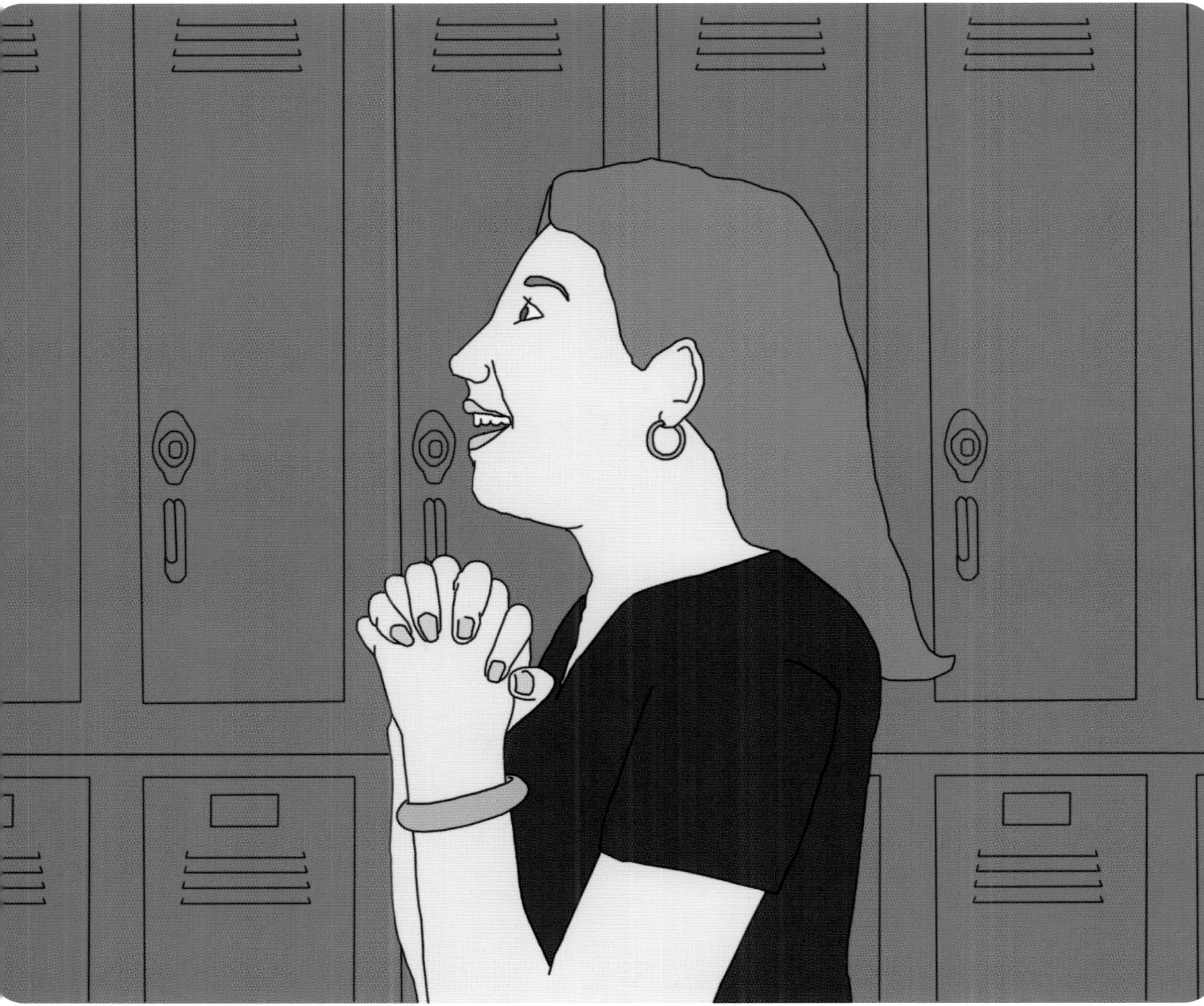

$\mathcal{T}$his could make her cool, maybe even prom queen next spring.

"Hey guys, check this out, you point to your jewelry and say...Bling Bling."

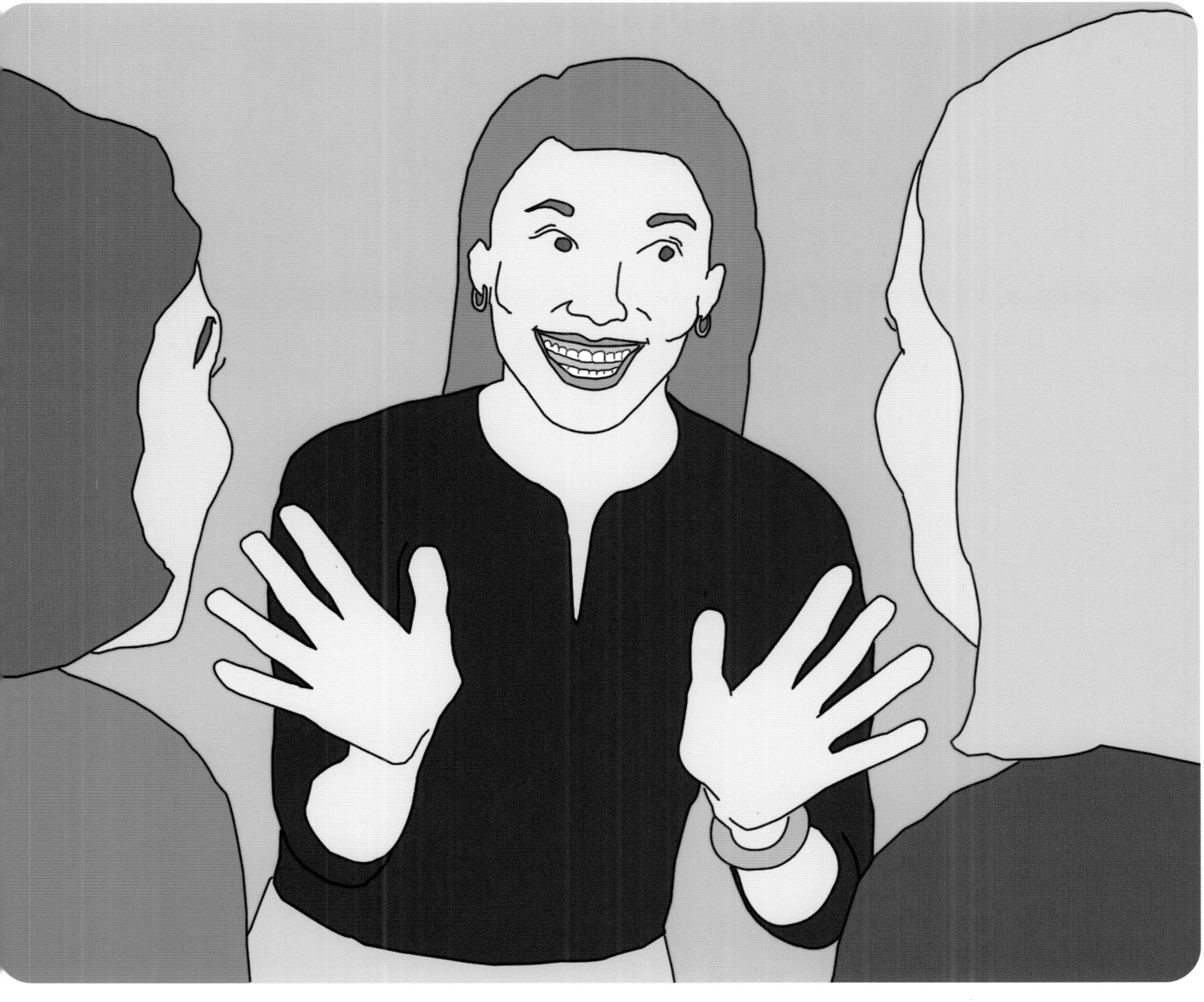

With this second group, it spread quicker than the first.

Except it sounded phony
and came off a little rehearsed.

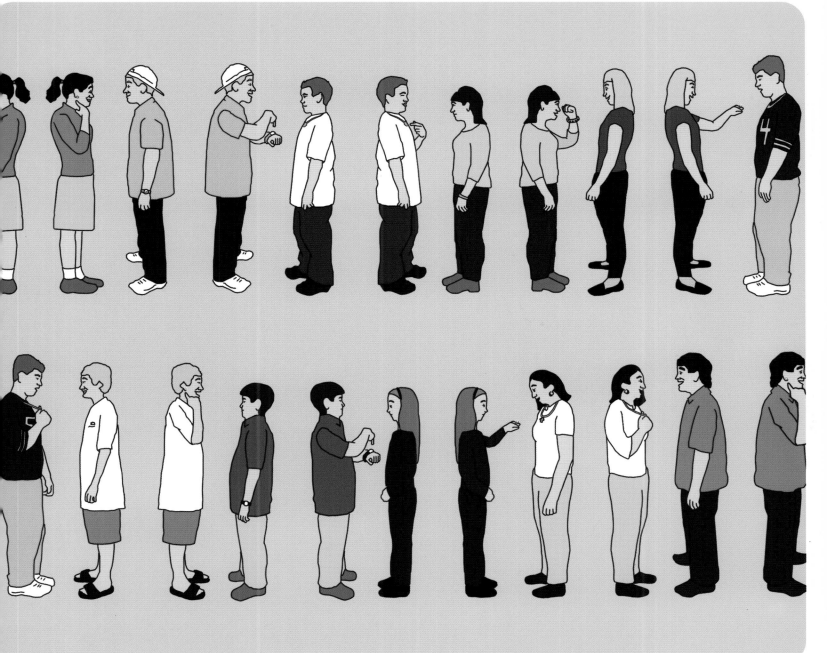

*T*ry as they did...to speak it from the heart...

It was totally unnatural,
they were just acting a part.

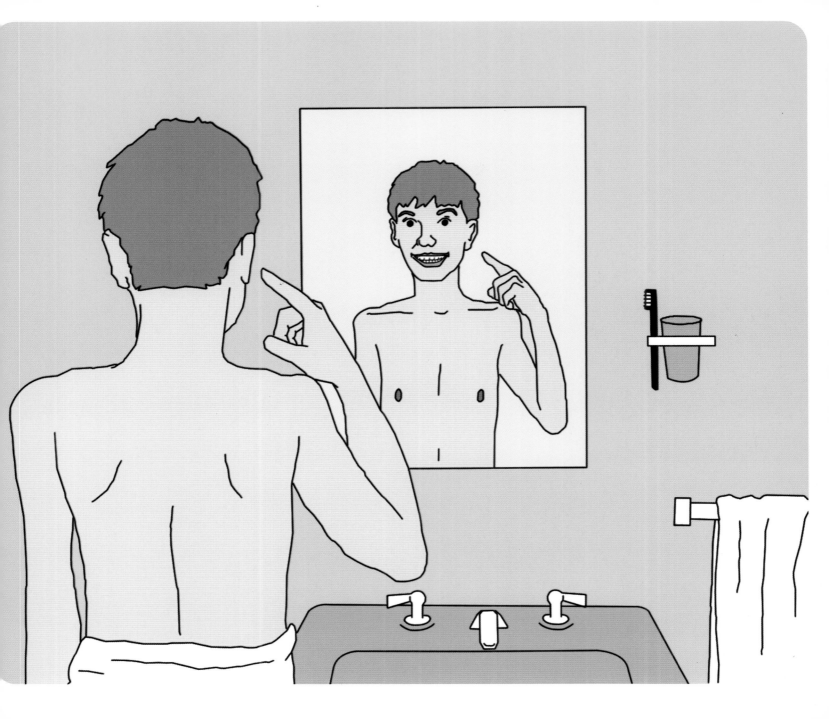

*N*ext came the most expected and damaging abuse.

Madison Avenue got wind of it
and realized it had commercial use.

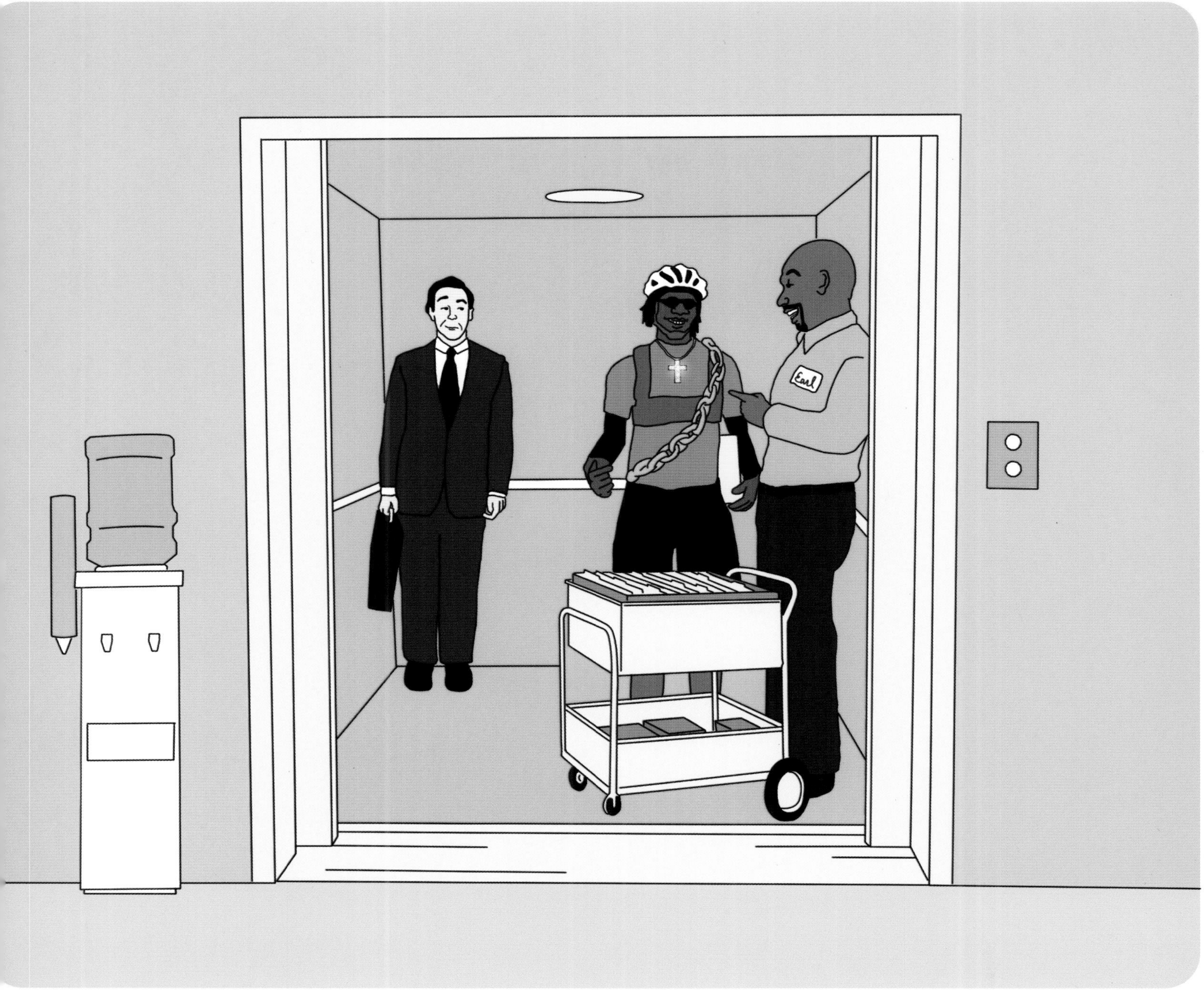
Earl

*A*s the adman pitched his client,
its demise was now in full swing.

"We can reach urban youths.

Have you heard this expression, Bling Bling?"

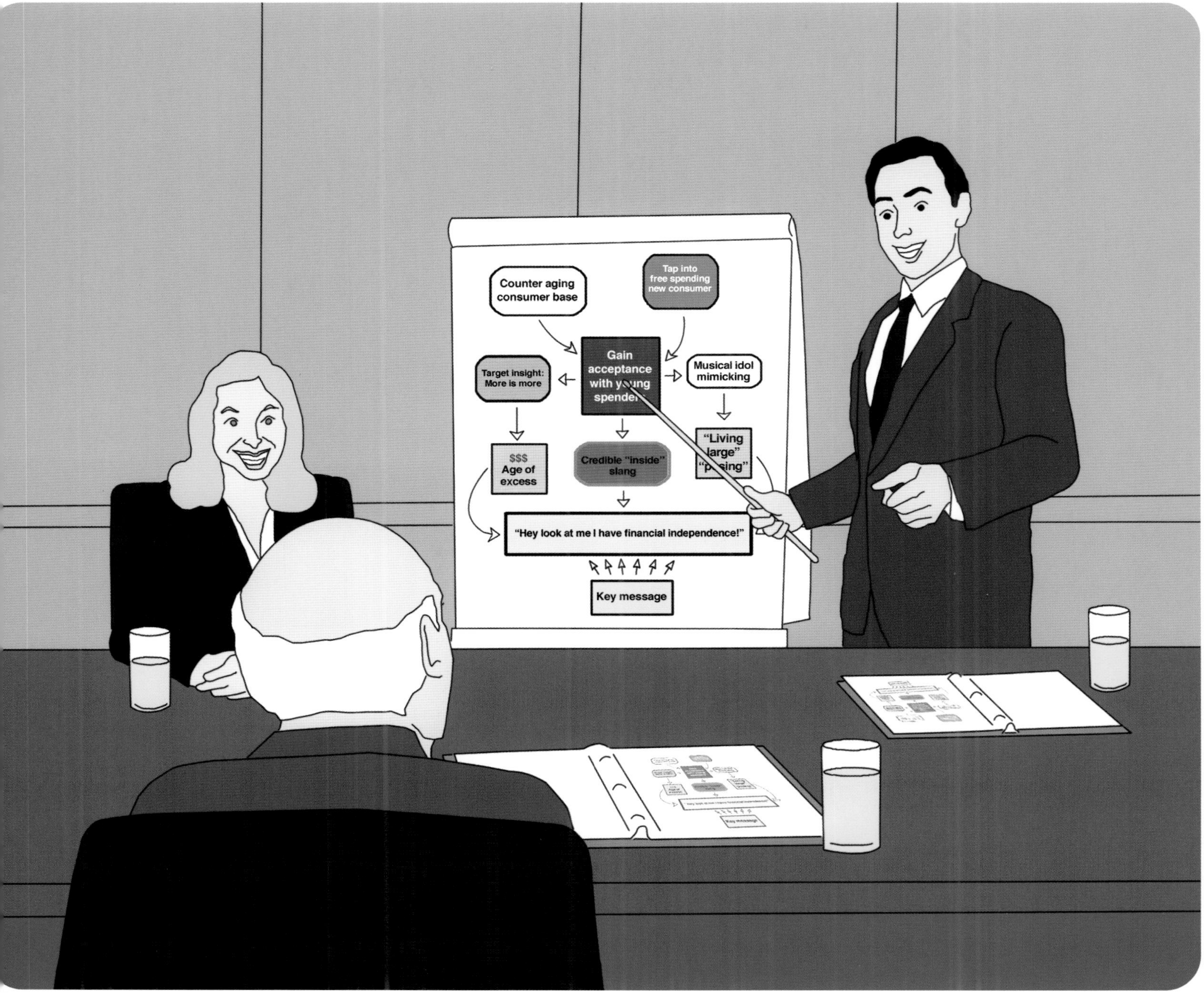
Counter aging consumer base
Tap into free spending new consumer
Gain acceptance with
Target insight: More is more
Musical idol mimicking
$$$ Age of excess
Credible "inside" slang
“Living large”
“Hey look at me I have financial independence!”
Key message

*N*ow out in the open exposed for all to see.

In the most foreign of lands—
a Pennysaver Circular on page 3.

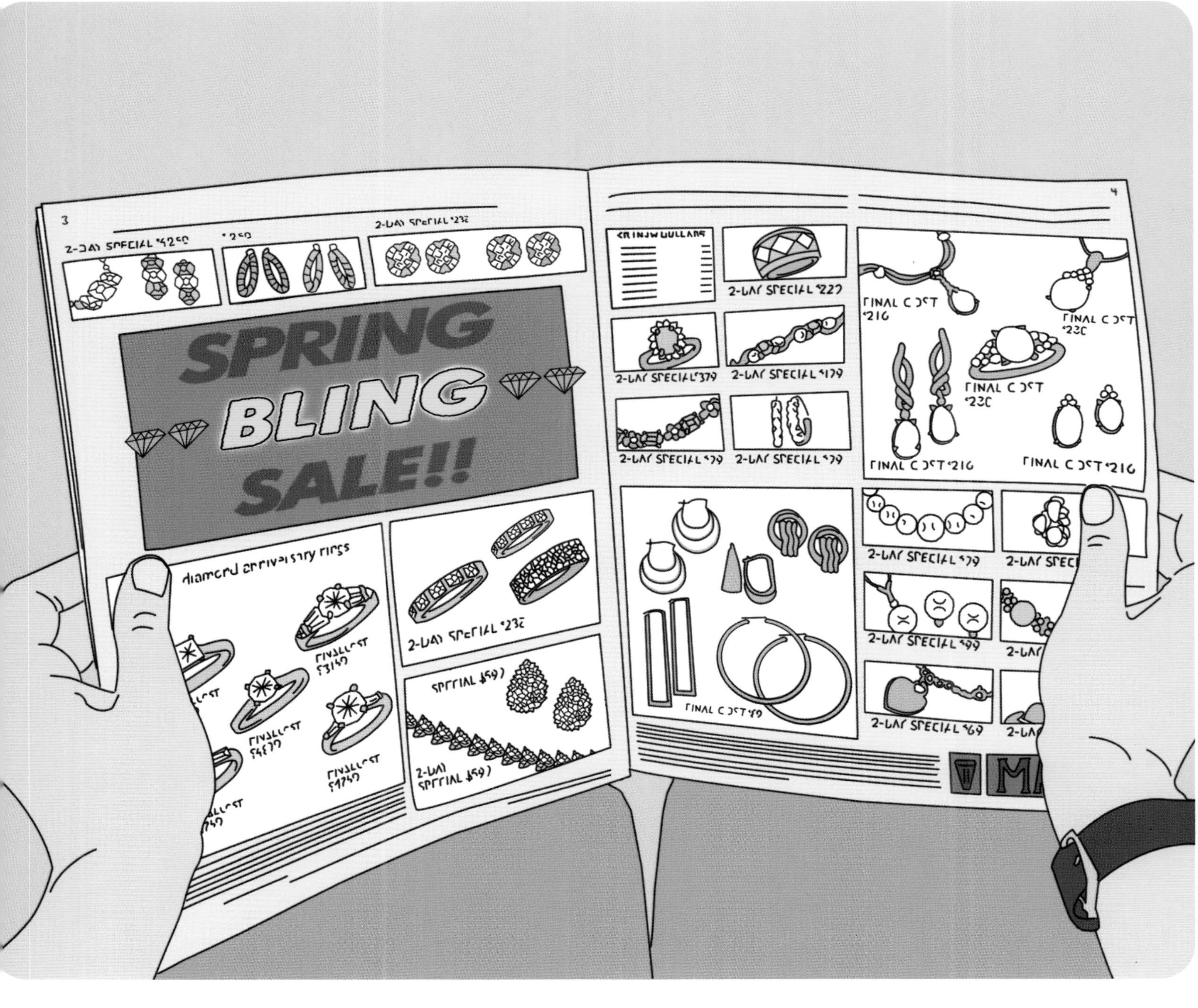
SPRING BLING SALE!!

*B*ling Bling was battered, it was obvious the end was near.

It came in the form of Sheila, wife of a custodial engineer.

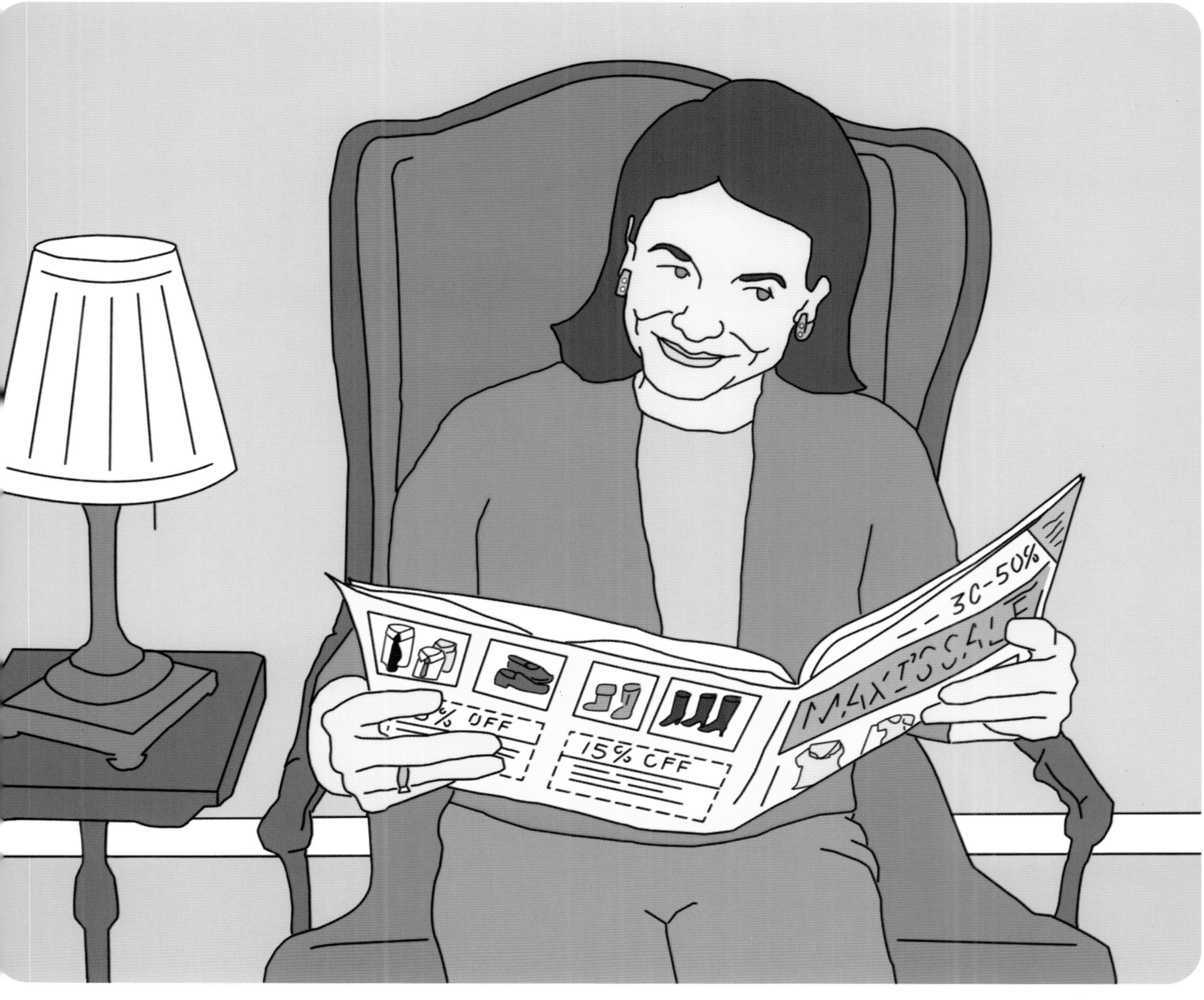
% OFF

*A*t her mother's to brag,
"I haggled these earrings 15% cheaper."

She was also there to play the part
of Bling Bling's grim reaper.

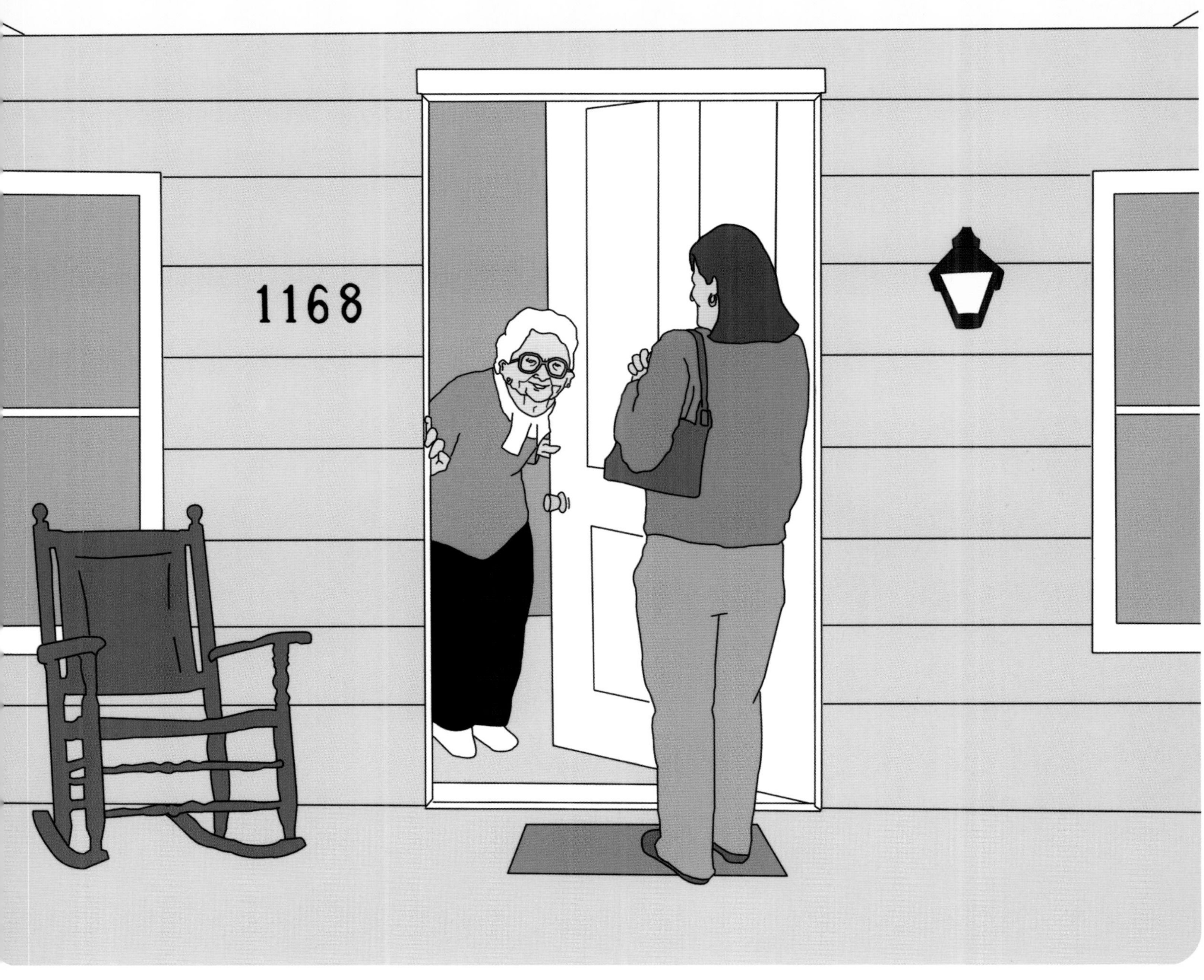
1168

$\mathcal{B}$y then it was like an injured bird
flopping on the ground with a broken wing.

Mercifully came the nail in the coffin...
Sheila pointed to her ears...and said..."Bling Bling."

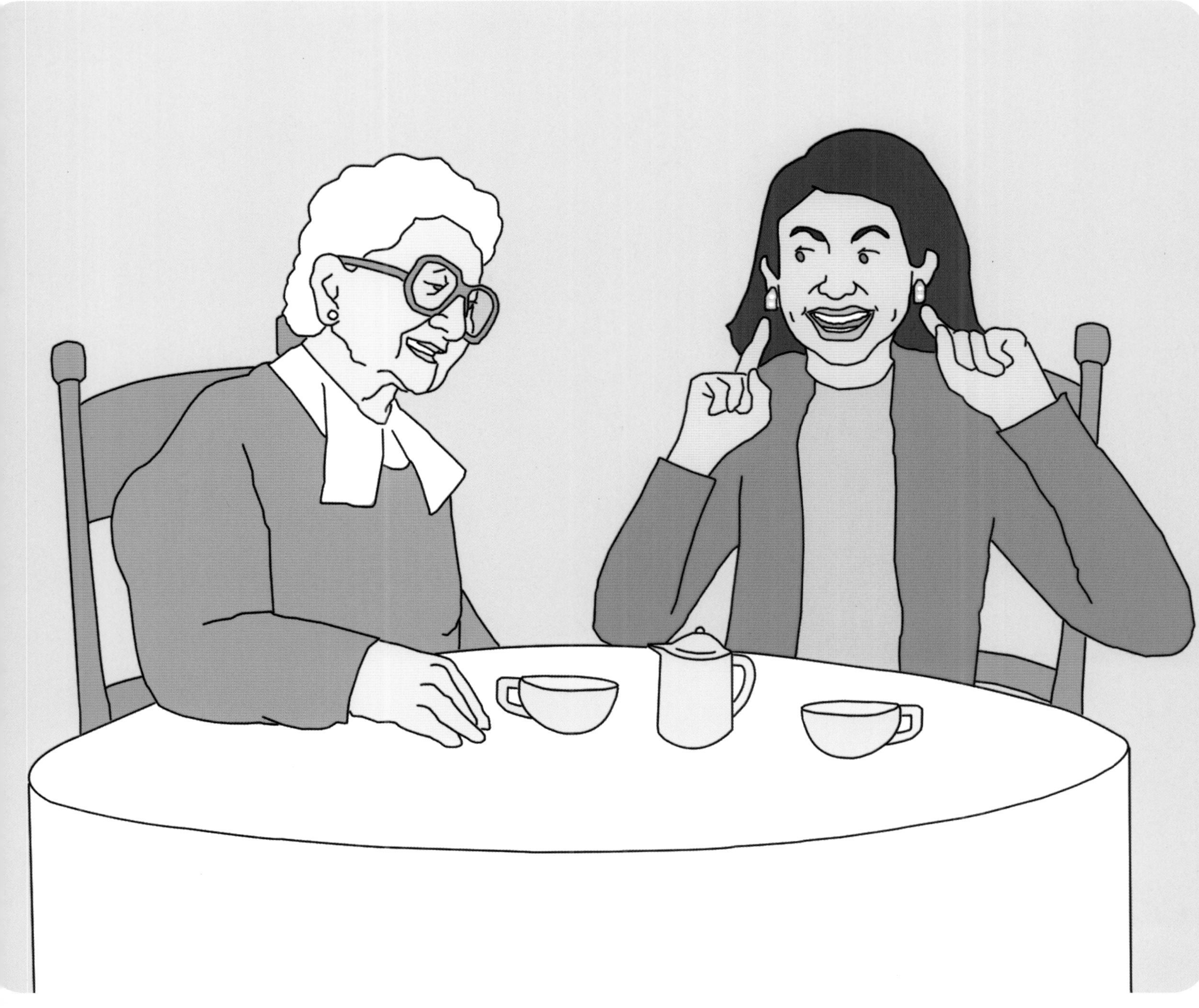

The End

(let's hope.)

Book design by Susan Hildebrand [Design] at susanhildebrand.com

Copyediting by Dan Rollman at snerko.com

Special thanks goes to:
Nancy Vescovo
Lola Ray Vescovo
Mr. Jorge Pinto
Ray Sternesky
Junior Mc Rae
Jenna Vescovo
Mikie Vescovo
Alaine Vescovo
Jordan Plitt
Eddie Plitt
Chelsea Moller
Juliet Dombrowski
Dominique Constantino
Heather Finn
Chris Leykam
Michael Sternesky
Tommy "Ghunz" Dudley
Cyril "KI" Morris
Michael Bellino
Amy Reichenthal

There's more learning to do.

INSTRUCTOART.COM

Matthew Vescovo: The Life and Death of BLING BLING

All images and text ©2004 Matthew Vescovo

Published by
Instructoart Book Associates, a partnership between Jorge Pinto Books and Instructo, LLC

Design and typesetting: Susan Hildebrand [Design]
Printed and bound in China by Toppan Printing Company, HK Limited
ISBN 0-9742615-2-1

Available through D.A.P./Distributed Art Publishers
155 Sixth Avenue, 2nd Floor, New York, NY 10013
Tel: (212) 627-1999 Fax: (212) 627-9484
Library of Congress Cataloging -in- Publication Data

Matthew Vescovo
The Life and Death of BLING BLING, a humorous account of the evolution of a popular catchphrase.